I0072385

TOP TIPS

for interactive skills in business

Quick reference tips
that will help you improve
your interactions with others
in business

Patricia Ryan

cSc

Communication Skills Consultancy
Lake Street
Cairns North Qld 4870
Australia
www.communicationskillsconsultancy.com.au

This book is copyright. Apart from any fair dealing for the purpose of private study, research, criticism or review, as permitted under the Copyright Act, no part may be reproduced by any process without written permission. Enquiries should be addressed to the Publishers.

All rights reserved.

Cataloguing-in-Publication entry available at National Library of Australia.

ISBN: 978-0-6451840-7-5 (paperback)
ISBN: 978-0-6451840-8-2 (ebook)

Published by Communication Skills Consultancy
in collaboration with DoctorZed Publishing
W: www.doctorzed.com
E: info@doctorzed.com

Printed in Australia, UK, and USA

rev. date 21/08/2021

Research tells us that 80% of the people who fail at work do so for one reason - they do not relate well to others.

And yet, how many businesses train their staff in interactive communication skills?

Many professional people will tell you that they thought their technical training was all they would need in their working environment; however they now find they spend many hours settling workplace disharmony and miscommunication.

Approximately half the work I do is done with management in companies and organisations advising and training them in interactive communication skills. When they realise the immense difference this training can mean to their different entities, they then call me in to train their staff as well.

Training in Interactive Skills produces results - not only in business resulting in improved relationships with clients and/or customers, but also with work colleagues.

The skills required to do this aren't so very difficult to learn.

In this Top Tips for Interactive Skills in Business, you will find succinct ways to travel this sometimes difficult but in the end, most satisfying road to success in communicating in business.

Dedication

To all managers, leaders, and staff
who endeavour to bring about
effective interactive
communication skills within their
working environment.

Contents

Owner and Director of the Communication Skills Consultancy, Patricia Ryan is an international presenter, qualified educator and facilitator, author, and an accredited trainer and assessor in all aspects of personal and business communication skills. She holds further various qualifications, including a Degree in Business Management, and studies in Professional Counselling; she is a past District Governor of Toastmasters International.

Her clients range from large businesses and corporations including Universities, Business Colleges, Commonwealth Government Departments, Police and Defence Force recruits through to management and staff of small and family entities. She is a consultant to various organisations while continuing to train, mentor and coach individuals.

Having had the affliction of stuttering for a large part of her life, interactive skills between people is a passion with her.

Besides speaking engagements, giving seminars, workshops, master classes, and presentations, as well as training others in communication skills, Patricia has, this past few years, put pen to paper, or should we say fingers to the keyboard, and writes on various aspects of her subject matter. Her previous books are Top Tips for Public Speaking and Top Tips for Interpersonal Communication.

She travels widely in her business and lives in Cairns North Queensland, after moving some years ago from Brisbane, Queensland, Australia.

"*For anyone in business, '*Top Tips for Interactive Skills In Business' *is an excellent resource... Patricia correctly identifies skills and foundations in communication that can be easily ignored, especially in our current society, where digital devices appear to monopolise the means and content of supposedly effective relationships.*"

John Hartigan Director
John Hartigan & Associates
Human Resources & Industrial Relations

"*Patricia Ryan's book, '*Top Tips for Interactive Skills in Business' *is a reference book that should be owned by every manager and potential manager in every organisation in the world. It should be kept within easy reach to allow for growth in that manager, or indeed, the staff that they 'manage.' A happy workplace is almost as essential as a happy home for a productive life, and happy staff are the foundation of that model. To achieve that, organisations need managers that have the skills that are outlined concisely in this book, which should be in every manager's armamentarium. Organisations with a stress-less workplace may be utopian, but '*Top Tips' *brings that closer. Most highly recommended.*"

Chris Shaw
Pharmacist and author

*T*o all the company's and organisations that I have been fortunate enough to work with - thank you for showing me how communication and interactive skills work best in business.

To all the CEO's who worked with me in improving their skills in communicating with their staff – thank you; and what a difference we made more often than not.

To my readers who edited my efforts and gave input – thank you; I'm sure the book is much better because of your kind efforts.

To my children Steven, Linda and Karen who inspire me every day, thank you so much.

&

Material for this book has been gathered over many years of study, teaching, writing and training others in interpersonal communication skills. This book has been compiled through the author's observations and experience.

'*T*o be agreeable, all that is necessary
is to take an interest in other persons
and in other things,
to recognise that other people as a rule
are much like one's self,
and thankfully to admit that diversity is a
glorious feature of life.'

Frank Swinnerton (b,1884-1982)
British novelist and critic

I believe communication in business starts with your work environment. Do you jump out of bed in the morning ready and enthusiastic to get to the business of the day, or do you struggle out bemoaning the fact that you have to go to work? It is right at that point in time that can make or break your day. Think about how you want to spend it; happy or grumpy.

How well you and your colleagues work together can make the difference between a successful organisation or a poor one.

Being able to deal with personality differences within the organisation is only a part of having effective interactive skills in business. We also need to be able to work within the team, at times being its leader, or perhaps you are a manager and need to concentrate on 'the bottom line' ensuring the company or organisation thrives and survives.

Solving problems, handling conflict and using mediation skills are all part and parcel of being able to interact effectively in business.

Social media and networking also play a large part in being successful in taking your business into the community. There is no area in which interactive and interpersonal communication is not a necessity.

'**Y**ou can close more business
in two months by becoming interested
in other people than you can
in two years trying to get people
interested in you.'

Dale Carnegie

Chapter 1

Interacting at Work
Getting Along with Colleagues
Personality Profiles
Emotional Intelligence
Workplace Values

'*D*on't find fault, find a remedy.'

Henry Ford (1863-1947)
American Automobile Manufacturer

*B*eing happy at work is a tremendous blessing. It means you will not only look forward to your working week but shouldn't suffer from headaches, aches and pains, depression and a host of other ailments. How to achieve that state is the question. There could be a simple answer or a particular situation may need in-depth analysis.

If we look at some basics of communication skills we find that we shouldn't criticise others, order them around, criticise them openly and in fact we are meant to care about others and understand shall we say, 'what makes them tick.' How often do you think we do this, and especially at work?

It is a fact that a happy workplace increases productivity and therefore delivers a better outcome for all concerned.

Throughout this book you will find many ideas, suggestions and processes to improve your interpersonal relationships, but for these couple of pages I'm starting with basics we all know but don't always use. The following Top Tips should bring about some light-bulb moments for you.

Some Fundamental Basics

Arriving at work with a smile on your face and a hello for everyone usually creates a friendly atmosphere.

While it's normally nice to get along with your colleagues try not to grizzle or complain about the weather, family or work.

A positive attitude often rubs off on others.

It's not always necessary if working in a large organisation to remember everyone's name, but necessary for those working in your department.

You can show your interest in others by enquiring as to how they are and/or follow up on any problems they may be facing.

It seems superfluous to mention some of these very basic things, but as I go into companies and businesses to assess their communication within the workplace I continually find they are lacking in these very basics.

Working with colleagues

Appreciate the persons you work with. Be courteous and give encouragement.

TOP TIPS:

- Your colleagues will be more productive if you show approval and appreciation
- Be a good listener
- Personal hygiene – you do wear deodorant don't you?
- Overdoing the perfume or aftershave can be uncomfortable for those working near you
- If others are encroaching on your work, speak to them about it
- If others are not doing their share or pulling their weight, assess if this is *your* problem before making a complaint; and/or try using an assertive message
- Gossip is always a no-no

If you really want to get along well with your colleagues, know what interests them.

It's always a good idea, as Dale Carnegie said many years ago, to 'make the other person feel important.' (This still works today). We can do this by asking their opinion or their ideas, and being interested in their answers.

12 Ways to winning people to our way of thinking

Once again, I mention Dale Carnegie in 'Winning People to our Way of Thinking', and have done up the twelve steps he (and others since) assure us work well. (I should add that I have trained many people in these steps even today, with excellent results, so try them yourself).

They are;

1. Avoid argument and confrontation. Nobody is ever convinced against their will.
2. Respect the other person's opinion. Never say "you're wrong." Best to let it lie for a moment then say what you thought and why. You will be surprised how quickly the other person will see your point of view.
3. If you are wrong, admit it quickly and emphatically.
4. Be friendly, and maintain a friendly manner.
5. Always emphasise the areas on which you and the other person agree.
6. Don't FORCE your ideas on others.
7. Let the other person do most of the talking.
8. Try to see the other person's point of view.
9. Be sympathetic to the other person's ideas and desires.
10. Appeal to a person's nobler motives. Assume that the other person is honest, sincere, and truthful.
11. Dramatise your ideas. Build a picture in their minds. Show them.
12. Offer a challenge.

We probably spend more hours at work than at home so it makes sense to try and enjoy those hours. And just imagine how great it would be to begin each work day with the same enthusiasm as we begin our days off, with a spring in our step because we like going to work!

As you can see, it is not so difficult to get along with your colleagues (and others as well) if you apply some simple steps or methods to everyday interactions.

TOP TIP

Think in terms of the other person's point of view

'*I*f you want to gather honey,
don't kick over the beehive.'

Dale Carnegie

*O*rganisations today often call in psychologists to do personality profiling on their prospective employees, to ascertain their expected behaviours, and whether that particular personality style and/or behaviour will fit in with the team.

To be an effective communicator, one of the first rules we must follow is not to label others. Another area we need to be careful of is not to judge others. So where does this leave personality profiling? By all means take personality tests – you can learn a lot about yourself and others by the focus you will need to place on your own behaviour and that of others – but keep them in perspective, as we are all individuals, with our own unique behaviour patterns.

It would fill more pages than this book has to delve into each type of possible personality style, which can range from 32 styles, down through 24, 16 or 12, until we come to a final four. For the purpose of these Top Tips, we will look at the main four types we can use as a base to improve our interaction with others. We can also observe some of the behaviours that pertain to ourselves; and how our own style may affect others' behaviours towards us.

The four basic styles that we can recognise in others (and hopefully ourselves) are: The Dominant/Driver; the Expressive/ Influencing; the Stable/Solid; and the Analytical/Compliant.

See if you can recognize the following styles:

DOMINANT/DRIVER PERSONALITY STYLE
◇   These people are active personalities.
◇   They like to be in control of any situation.
◇   They are goal and results oriented.
◇   Can be opinionated and blunt.
◇   Can be decisive and controlling.
◇   Can be impatient.
◇   They enjoy challenges.

Dominant/Driver – Personal Behaviour

◇ They can be competitive.
◇ Determined, demanding.
◇ Driving, responsible.
◇ Strong-willed, independent.
◇ Ambitious, logical.

Dominant/Driver – Possible weaknesses

◇ Can overstep authority.
◇ Have an argumentative attitude.
◇ Can attempt too much at once.
◇ Can be blunt; stubborn.
◇ Dislike routine.

Ways to communicate with Dominant/Drivers

They respond best if we are specific in our communication.

TOP TIPS:

• Present facts logically
• Persuade by referring to objectives and results
• Show your support
• Provide choices
• Offer them new challenges

EXPRESSIVE/INFLUENCING PERSONALITY STYLE

◇ These people are active personalities.
◇ Need approval and like compliments.
◇ Enthusiastic, motivational.
◇ Persuasive, talkative.
◇ Impulsive, emotional.
◇ Make fast decisions.
◇ Trusting, friendly.

Expressive/Influencing – Personal Behaviour

◇ Sociable, popular.
◇ Persuasive, expressive.

◇ Enthusiastic, confident.
◇ Freedom from controls and details.
◇ Independent, optimistic.

Expressive/Influencing – Possible weaknesses
◇ Can need approval and compliments.
◇ Can generalise too much.
◇ Inattentive to detail.
◇ Can tend to listen only when it's convenient.
◇ Can be opinionated, biased.

Ways to communicate with Expressive /Influencing Types
Use language that encompasses feelings. Ask their advice.

TOP TIPS:
• Recognise their accomplishments, pay them a compliment
• Don't bore them with too many details and facts-based logic
• Share with them your own ideas
• Be friendly, chat with them

STABLE/SOLID PERSONALITY STYLE
◇ These people are generally passive personalities.
◇ They are good listeners and like people.
◇ They are steady, predictable.
◇ They are supportive.
◇ They are understanding, friendly.
◇ Counsellor types - help others.
◇ Compliant towards authority.

Stable/Solid – Personal Behaviour
◇ Reliable, dependable.
◇ Possessive.
◇ Patient, empathetic.
◇ Good at reconciling conflicts.
◇ Predictable, systematic.
◇ Loyal.

Stable/Solid – Possible weaknesses

- ◇ Dislike change.
- ◇ Can be insecure – need reassurance.
- ◇ Can hold a grudge.
- ◇ Sensitive to criticism.
- ◇ Dislike conflict.
- ◇ Don't take risks.

Ways to communicate with Stable/Solid Types

Recognise their loyalty and dependability.

TOP TIPS:

- Be informal, orderly and friendly
- Show sincere interest in them
- Ask "how" questions
- Don't enter into conflict or argument with them

ANALYTICAL/COMPLIANT PERSONALITY STYLE

- ◇ These people are passive personalities.
- ◇ They are planners and organizers.
- ◇ They are problem-solvers.
- ◇ Accurate, analytical.
- ◇ Precise, logical.
- ◇ Conscientious, detailed.

Analytical/Compliant – Personal Behaviour

- ◇ They concentrate on the detail, technicalities.
- ◇ Can be slow in making decisions.
- ◇ Persistent, persevering.
- ◇ Follow procedures.
- ◇ Thorough, systematic.
- ◇ Conservative and cautious.

Analytical/Compliant – Possible weaknesses

◇ Must be right.
◇ Need clear cut boundaries for actions and relationships.
◇ Prefer not to verbalise feelings.
◇ Bound by procedures and methods.
◇ Get bogged down in details.

Ways to communicate with Analytical/Compliant Types

These people will appreciate it if you converse with them in a straightforward but low key manner.

TOP TIPS:

• Acknowledge their logical, methodical approach to most things
• Explain things to them in detail
• Keep clear of conflicts
• Give these people practical procedures and routine
• Keep social interaction limited

It is very probable that you have ticked boxes in all of the personality style behaviours – this is quite normal; after all, it is highly unlikely that we can compartmentalise ourselves and others into four personality types. This is where a full personality profile analysis can divide your style (and others) into where we are strongest and where we are weakest.

For the purposes of interacting with others; just having an overall knowledge of behavioural styles not only of ourselves but also of others, gives us some tools to interact more effectively, personally and professionally.

Generally, if you can learn to respond to each behavioural type, you will develop rapport with that person.

TOP TIP

Our behaviour style affects our communication

'**B**y questioning the rules of others
and the rules we have taken
into our reality,
we have new options and choices.'

Influencing with Integrity, Genie Z Laborde

*T*he expression *emotional intelligence* or *EI* indicates a kind of intelligence or skill that involves the ability to perceive, assess and positively influence one's own and other people's emotional state of being.

Emotional Intelligence (EI) is not the same as our IQ (Intelligence Quotient). A person can have a high IQ but a low EI and vice versa.

Emotional Intelligence is a type of personal and social intelligence which includes:

◇ Emotional awareness – the ability to perceive, recognise, understand and react to the feelings of yourself and others.
◇ Emotional literacy – the ability to distinguish between various feelings and to name them.
◇ Emotional control – the ability to express and control our feelings appropriately.
◇ The ability to listen to others, to have empathy with them and to interact effectively in terms of emotions and thoughts.
◇ The ability to use this information in directing our thoughts and actions; recognising the relationship between thoughts, feelings and behaviours.

To ascertain your level of Emotional Awareness, go to Appendix 1 and answer the questionnaire.

Feelings and emotions

Feelings are internal, we perceive them through our senses, and then interpret them. We then use behaviour to communicate those feelings.

All emotions are forms of energy. Feelings of love and anger for example, can generate energy which allows us to behave in a certain way.

Feelings are the one trait we all have that gives us a sense of community, and can be consciously or unconsciously generated. The environment (socialisation) and our genetic make-up both play a role in the origin of feelings.

TOP TIPS:
- The better we understand our own feelings, the better we can understand those of others
- We cannot enjoy feelings if we are unaware of them
- We cannot express feelings if we suppress or ignore them
- Our emotions do not only happen in our head; our whole body is involved and influenced

Accepting feelings/emotions
- ◇ To accept our feelings, we need to be aware of them and accept them as our own.
- ◇ Don't let experiencing strong feelings frighten you. If we don't fully accept them, we will never learn what they are, where they come from, and what the cause was.
- ◇ We may blame ourselves or others, or feel sad about feelings we do not accept.
- ◇ People who are unable to accept their own feelings blame others for their anger, or they convince themselves that their feelings of sadness and anxiety are something to be ashamed of.
- ◇ Difficult feelings that are only experienced in part are distorted. This wastes time and energy and blurs our senses.
- ◇ Acceptance of our feelings shows we are able to cope with any feeling irrespective of its intensity.
- ◇ Humour and laughter are worthy tools in the acceptance of feelings.
- ◇ Acceptance makes it easier to laugh at our mistakes.
- ◇ Laughing brings us into our body – it is like exercise for the inner being.

Experiencing Feelings/Emotions
- ◇ We have to be able to experience, accept and enjoy positive feelings.

◇ Are you able to experience, accept and enjoy feelings of excitement, sensuality and love for more than just a few minutes?
◇ Let yourself enjoy the pleasant feeling and let it intensify by deep breathing and experiencing it in full in your body.
◇ The reward for emotional acceptance is more intense positive feelings that last longer, and more intense unpleasant feelings that are quickly dissipated.

Consequences of not accepting our feelings

◇ Feelings that are not experienced and accepted may lead to physical symptoms such as stomach pains, migraine, back pain, stiff neck, ulcers, regular colds, asthma, and insomnia. Ignoring or repressing feelings can lead to compulsive behaviour, e.g. smoking, drinking, drug use, overworking, overeating, over exercising, and other obsessive/addictive behaviours.
◇ We can say and do the wrong things at the wrong times, or don't say no to anything!
◇ We can cut off feelings and rationalise, think of excuses, or lose contact with reality.

The lessons in feelings

Feelings are signals for our body to determine what is right and what our needs are. Sometimes we can experience a feeling incorrectly, as a result of our interpretation or our automatic response patterns (the behaviours we don't think about). It is our responsibility to verify what the reality is. Feelings motivate us to examine the past, to feel the present and to find a different path in the future.

TOP TIPS:

• Each emotion is to tell us that we need to give attention to something
• We can differentiate between positive and negative feelings, and it is important to know that a negative feeling is valuable because it indicates an unmet need. It is therefore essential that we do not suppress negative emotions

- Feelings are meant to motivate us, to have us ask questions, and to act in order to change something
- The more passion we have about something, the more motivated we are to do something about it
- It is usually the strongest emotions that spur us on. How many great performances are frequently the result of frustration?
- Each person has a different emotional energy level reflected in their personalities – for example, cautious, relaxed, spontaneous, withdrawn, slow or quick – and they will react differently to each other
- Feelings are contagious. One depressed person in a family or working environment can influence others negatively
- Strive for balance between feelings and reason; neither is more important than the other - they should be in balance

Choosing our feelings

The information we gather through our senses – sight, hearing, smell, taste and touch, is interpreted in terms of our values, assumptions, and previous experiences. Although this process is not always conscious, we do have a choice in how we interpret this information. We can decide from which point of view we want to look at certain information.

- ◇ We give control to others when we think that they are causing our feelings; e.g. when we say "you are making me angry."
- ◇ The way we interpret (think about) the information we receive determines to a large degree our feelings about it. We can control our feelings by controlling our interpretation i.e. how we perceive a situation; our behaviour will then not be an impulsive reaction because we have thought about it logically.
- ◇ We have that choice about how we want to behave.

Enhancing Emotional Awareness

We can all learn to increase our emotional intelligence. The following activities may help to enhance your emotional awareness;

TOP TIPS:

- Keep a journal of your feelings. Indicate which situation gives rise to which feeling and what your reactions are. Become aware of the physical symptoms – stiff neck, sweating, heart palpitations etc. What emotion are you experiencing?
- Draw up a list of roles you have and determine the feelings that are associated with each role. For example, employee (frustration), housewife (fulfilment), student (anxiety) etc.
- Try to generate feelings; in this way you can imagine which feelings you will experience in which situation and what your reaction will be. If you have to deliver a presentation, experience the situation and feelings beforehand in a safe place through visualisation
- By keeping a journal of your dreams, you can become aware of unprocessed feelings in your subconscious mind. It is the feeling in your dreams that are important and not the situation in which they occur
- You can plan to fulfil your unmet needs when you see a pattern in your feelings. We tend to overemphasise our negative feelings and to see our positive feelings as less important. Make sure that you indicate your positive feelings as well, as these point to your fulfilled needs, which you need to keep and build on as part of your life

Values and Beliefs/Assumptions

Our values affect our thoughts, feelings and behaviours. We hardly ever think about what those values are, and how they determine our lives, but if we could define our values as to which bring happiness and fulfilment against which bring negative results, we could improve our lives accordingly.

One way to identify our values is by answering questions such as, "What am I striving for?" "What do I regard as important?" and "What guides my life?"

A person's assumptions, preconceptions and prejudices can be described as our 'truth'; our beliefs about how things work and ought to work. These convictions are learnt from early childhood and form a large part of our make-up.

You could ask yourself questions about what you believe in, or "What do I believe about relationships, my rights, the world?" If we examine our beliefs and discover some that are detrimental to our growth, they can be changed.

Our values and beliefs play an important role in the way we look at and experience life. The better we understand our values, beliefs and assumptions, the better we are able to have more fulfilling and rewarding relationships.

TOP TIPS:

- Write down ten values that are important to you; tick the values that bring about positive feelings, and mark with a cross the values that lead to negative feelings
- Now bring them down to 5. Can you narrow this down to the most important 3? How much time do you give those 3?
- Question your beliefs. Ask yourself, "What do I believe about" e.g. 'my rights,' 'relationships,' 'the roles I play,' 'trust,' 'how to handle problems,' 'rules,' (or whatever)
- Be prepared to change your views and expectations about life if that will make you feel more fulfilled

Self-Knowledge and Acceptance

Do you really know who you are and what you want?

When we know ourselves, we know what our values and needs are. We know which aspects of ourselves we are willing to make compromises about, and what we can't and don't want to change without giving up on ourselves. We realise and enjoy the fact that we are unique, special and immeasurable.

How we see ourselves (i.e. our self image), has an impact on others. If we see ourselves as failures, so will others; if we see ourselves as successful, so will others.

The picture we have of ourselves comes from two sources: the first is the feedback we receive from those we trust – parents, partners, significant others; the second is from our behaviour, abilities and experiences.

Going through the below Top Tips and putting into practice those that suit you will improve your self-knowledge and acceptance.

TOP TIPS:

- Don't compare yourself to others
- Identify and focus on your strengths and positive traits as well as areas for growth
- Be responsible for your own happiness and feelings. Consciously choose to be happy
- Take risks and be prepared to make mistakes
- Part of a person's emotional intelligence is reflected in their willingness to learn from their mistakes. Be persistent
- Don't try to be perfect and don't expect perfection from others
- Accept and make peace with yourself – physically and emotionally

Emotional Intelligence requires us to be aware of our feelings and those of others, to recognise that certain feelings cause certain reactions, which in turn can produce certain behaviours, and to understand that behaviours can stem from our values and beliefs.

The benefits of being emotionally intelligent allow us to recognise our own feelings and those of others; know the difference between thoughts, feelings and behaviours, and find a balance between expressing and controlling our feelings.

We can use this information to live more effectively, be motivated (and have a goal in mind). Because we can empathise with others, this improved communication leads to healthier relationships. Emotional 'baggage' can be left behind, allowing us to progress towards a happier and more fulfilling life.

TOP TIP

Being emotionally intelligent improves our interaction with others

CASE STUDY
I.Q. [Intelligence Quotient] OR E.I. [Emotional Intelligence]

A straight 'A' student at a high school in Florida was fixated on getting into medical school; not just any medical school – he dreamt of Harvard.

However, his physics teacher had given him an 80 on a quiz – which related to a B.

Believing the grade - a mere B - put his dream in jeopardy, Jason took a knife to school and, in a confrontation with the teacher, stabbed him in the collarbone, before being subdued in a struggle.

A judge found Jason innocent, temporarily insane during the incident – a panel of four psychologists and psychiatrists swore he was psychotic during the fight.

After transferring to another school, Jason graduated two years later at the top of his class.

Even as Jason graduated with highest honours, his old physics teacher complained that Jason had never apologised or even taken responsibility for the attack on him two years earlier.

The question is – how could someone of such obvious intelligence do something so irrational – so downright stupid?

Answer: Think on it... what do you believe?

Excerpt from Daniel Coleman's book '*Emotional Intelligence*'.

*P*lace the following workplace values in order of their importance to you.

Acceptance: These people want to be part of the team; to feel like an equal, be in on information as soon as it's out there, and generally feel a sense of belonging.

Accomplishment: These people love it when the job is done and there's a finished product. Taking something from nothing, working through it all the way and not giving up; they're often the person who adds the finishes to projects and/or reports.

Autonomy: These persons place a high value on being accountable to self over others. They like to work at their own pace, free from supervisors. They prefer to be fully responsible and accountable.

Competence: These people have a strong emphasis on knowledge, skills, and training. They like to do the job right the first time and expect others to do the same. They can be quick to complain if they feel someone is falling short on their responsibilities.

Control: These persons need to know all the details; it's important to them to orchestrate every aspect of larger projects. They are able to see the big picture, but can get bogged down in details.

Cooperation: Sharing of information, tasks, and details to further the ends of the organisation is what these people consider the most important value. They believe people are better and more successful working together.

Recognition: These people place a high value on giving and receiving credit for a job well done. They thrive on compliments, and may have many awards and certificates on their walls. A pat on the back goes a long way with them as it is not always just knowing that they did a good job, but that others also know.

Respect: Respect in the workplace can be acknowledging someone's expertise, validating a person's contribution, or simply not stealing someone's lunch from the refrigerator. Those who value respect treat others in a way that doesn't diminish their self-worth.

How someone reacts to a situation can give you a clue about their values. Think about how your fellow workers react to different situations and ascertain the value that is important to them.

Remember that values are unique to each individual so be careful of assuming you automatically identified the right value for a co-worker.

Don't be afraid to let co-workers know of your values. It may help them to relate to you in a manner conducive to better communication.

TOP TIP

Our values often dictate our behaviour

Chapter 2

Interacting within the Community
Networking
Electronic Media
Business Relationships
Culture and Communication

'*T*here are no limitations
to the mind except
those we acknowledge.
Both poverty and riches
are the offspring
of thought.'

Napoleon Hill
Think & Grow Rich

'It's not who you know, but who knows you!'
That's the networking mantra.

*I*f we are to become visible and build our profile, whether we like it or not, we need to network. That means moving out of our office and out into the public arena. Be aware though that networking can cost money, takes time, and needs planning. Therefore we need to ascertain just how much networking we need, or want to do, to obtain the results we are looking for. It is important to plan your networking, cost-wise and time-wise.

If you are new to networking, try attending a couple of events just to observe how others do it. You will find by the third time you attend (or even before) someone will say, "Hello, what do you do?" You don't have to come across all hale and hearty unless you feel comfortable in that role.

Take your time, observe, seek out another person who may be looking as timid as you feel and approach them.

Planning

Plan your year by responding to the following questions:-

- ◇ What do I want to accomplish networking-wise?
- ◇ How many functions or events can I attend?
  (One a week? One a month? Two a month?)
- ◇ Why this function?
- ◇ Who will be there?
- ◇ How will this function benefit my business?

The function or event

Think about what material you should take to this function that will build your profile.

Check with the organisers if you will be able to place your material in the room for easy access by attendees? Ask yourself the following questions;

◇ Who will I be able to present my material to?
◇ Is the function an opportunity to expand my circle of contacts?
◇ Will I meet people whose services or knowledge I can draw upon in the future?

Systems

One of the first things to look at is your name tag. Get used to having it in your bag or pocket to wear at all functions.

◇ Business cards; does your card tell what you do?
◇ Use a diary/calendar.
◇ Data-bases – after the event, enter cards received into a data base with information you require; e.g. *where, when, what interested them, and anything else you might need in the future.* Maybe they have a preference for how they like to be contacted - phone, email, sms.

Personal

It goes without saying that your dress or attire says what you want it to say about you. Hopefully that's *not* scruffy or uncaring.

Do remember the deodorant.

First impressions count – what image do you want to portray?

Social skills

Smile. Look approachable and be friendly.

TOP TIPS:

• Practice your introduction, *e.g. "My name is ... I am a ... specialising in ..."* Keep it short and to the point. Don't give a self-promoting commercial
• Take an interest in others
• Listen – actively
• Keep an open mind
• Don't gossip!
• Give your attention to the person speaking
• Be careful with drinking limit
• Move around the room talking with different people

Follow ups

◇ Send a thank you to those who have given you information or assistance.

◇ Do up a newsletter and send out periodically.

◇ Email specific contacts who you would like to follow up with.

◇ Make contact with those in your data-base every two to three months.

General tips

◇ Always act in a professional manner.

◇ Constantly expand your network. Join new groups, do new things.

◇ Be reliable and punctual. If you say you will contact someone further, or introduce them to another, do so.

◇ Maintain an abundance mindset. Believe there is room for everyone.

Networking is not just something we do when we want something! It's not meant to be done at the precise moment you run out of clients. It needs to be a constant in your monthly schedule.

Belonging to a regular networking group is well worth the effort. Keeping in touch with like-minded people and going to other networking events lifts your profile and brings in more business!

Don't forget those business cards, and make sure they say what you do!

Things I can do to improve my networking skills

....

....

....

TOP TIP

It's not who you know but who knows you!

'One phone call is worth a thousand emails.'

Stephen Oberg

*T*oday, business is more often than not, run and done per electronic mediums. If this is not your modus operandi then you may not be up to date with what's happening in the business world today, and it might be a good idea to update your skills.

Electronic media has also spawned a whole new area in marketing, advertising and interviews being done online.

Marketing on line

There are numerous marketeers and companies who can organise and write you programs to advance your business so I won't bore you with details of the how, why, when etc. - suffice to say that you will still need to check your communication methods to include the values that your organisation or business stands for. Some Top Tips could be;

TOP TIPS:

- Check that the person or company you intend to use for your marketing knows and understands your business
- You and your marketeer need to 'be on the same page', so to speak
- If doing your own marketing, check out how others are doing it, and the results they have achieved
- Be aware that if your marketing creates a large increase in business, you need to be able to handle it

Interviewing on line

Communicating on line per interview requires that we think carefully on the words we intend to use, remembering people will remember just seven percent of those words. Your appearance and body language also needs to be taken into consideration in how the viewer will perceive you.

TOP TIPS:

- Skills in public speaking will be a massive advantage – so take some classes if necessary
- Be aware your body language will be spotlighted and needs to be open and friendly
- Words need to be enunciated clearly and rate of speaking is best slowed a little to allow for understanding and cogitation of audience

Social Media for Business

This area has really taken off in the past few years; there are, however some sites that allow personal gossip to encroach on the page. While social media does allow us to be more personal it is best to stay away from anything that could be detrimental to your company or organisation.

TOP TIPS:

- Stay on message – don't get carried away with too much irrelevant information
- Keep your messages business oriented. These sites are not for general gossip
- Return incoming messages as soon as possible – as you would with other incoming mail
- Be helpful to others. Your assistance will be appreciated and help your profile

Love it or hate it, social media is here to stay, and grow, and be used in our business dealings. How we handle this can make or break our credibility.

I notice many small business owners are now following the lead of big business and using professional marketing persons to handle their on-line marketing and henceforth their image. When hiring such a person or organisation it is wise to ensure you both share similar values and beliefs.

TOP TIP

Electronic media still requires interpersonal skills

'I fear the day that technology will surpass our human reaction. The world will have a generation of idiots.'

Albert Einstein

The Builders

All are architects of Fate.
Working in these walls of Time;
Some with massive deed and great,
Some with ornaments of rhyme

Nothing useless is, or low;
Each thing in its place is best;
And what seems but idle show
Strengthens and supports the rest

For the structure that we raise,
Time is with materials filled;
Our todays and yesterdays
Are the blocks with which we build.

Let us do our work as well,
Both the unseen and the seen;
Make the house where gods may dwell
Beautiful, entire, and clean,

Else our lives are incomplete
Standing in these walls of Time,
Broken stairways, where the feet
Stumble as they seek to climb.

Build today, then, strong and sure,
With a firm and ample base;
And ascending and secure
Shall tomorrow find its place.

Henry Wadsworth Longfellow
(excerpt)

*I*f we are in business, how well we handle the relationships we build with other business people, as well as the relationships we have with our staff, clients and/or customers, can spell the difference between success or failure.

Our attitude plays a big part in how we approach these relationships. For instance, the salesman who thinks about how to serve his customers will have a better result than the salesman who thinks the customer is there for his benefit.

If our attitude is about 'giving' rather than 'receiving,' it stands to reason that we should have many customers wanting our service or product.

Staff

Good staff relationships will increase the success of your business. If your employees are happy, your clients/customers will be happy! Giving staff the opportunity for input will increase their commitment.

How we treat our staff will show in their attitude to our client/ customers. Think about it, if you are cranky and demanding, chances are that your staff will treat customers much the same.

Perhaps your staff has ideas on how to improve the way things are done.

TOP TIPS:

- Have you thought on ways to improve staff satisfaction? If you ask, it is quite possible they will tell you. If they are dissatisfied, do you know why?
- Ask your staff for feedback. Listen to what they say and carry out if possible; if not, tell them why
- What are their needs? Get to know your staff
- Give positive support
- Deal with conflict *(see Ch.3)*
- Reward your staff for positive effort/outcomes

Clients

How do we stay in touch? Do our clients require regular contact or not so regular contact? You could also ask how they wish to be contacted; newsletters? phone calls? emails? Text? Knowing the answers to these questions can improve our relationship with clients immensely.

TOP TIPS:

- Listen to what clients/customers have to say about your organisation
- Invite client feedback
- Send Christmas wishes
- What about birthday messages?
- Would offering client discounts bring in more business?

Customers

Is our main concern for our customers, or the bottom line? Are we more concerned with our sales pitch? Or do we allow them to choose the goods they wish to buy with our assistance, and not persistence?

Recently I had to interrupt a sales person to ask, "Could I tell you what I want please, before you give me your sales pitch?"

TOP TIPS:

- Try to establish rapport so you can understand your customer's needs
- Check on how well customers are served
- Act on customer complaints
- Obtain feedback – per questionnaires, personal enquiry, follow-ups
- Think of ways to make contact with customers on a regular basis

Prospective clients

It's obvious I would think that if we are to attract new clients we need to go where we can meet them, hence networking events.

Secondly, when they come to us we need to immediately present a friendly and helpful attitude.

Talk with them about their needs, ask questions, then listen and listen some more. What could we offer them that will be of benefit to them and their organisation or company?

TOP TIPS:
- What are their expectations of your services?
- What are your expectations?
- Do we know the values they adhere to?
- What would be their core beliefs?
- Are they a people-oriented company or task oriented?

Associates and/or other businesses

Too often I feel that we are so concerned about our own needs that we believe all others are our adversaries. If we can change that thinking to one of assistance and support to all we will be surprised how work seems to come to us more often.

TOP TIPS:
- Have 'abundance' thinking – there is room for all of us
- Give freely of your assistance should you be asked
- Build positive support networks
- Say thank you to those who have helped you
- Acknowledge referrals
- Give referrals

Attitude

Having a positive and forward thinking attitude will remind you not to assume continuity (things won't always stay the same).

Beware of believing your own publicity, and/or praise from others. Those thoughts may be inspiring but can lead you to forget to keep moving forward.

TOP TIPS:
- Keep your promises
- Be clear on your obligations
- Maintain a 'service' approach to all dealings
- Look at criticisms as a challenge to improve
- Stay true to your integrity

The commercial imperative

It's old, but still holds true today – 'The customer is always right, even when they are wrong!'

If we are to interact with others it is wise to understand that people have different expectations, assumptions and perceptions about things, depending on their perspective, so be open to other opinions and prejudices.

TOP TIPS:
- Communication breakdowns cause ineffectiveness and mistakes
- Poor relationships cause poor morale and a lack of sharing transparency
- Arguing is a non-value adding activity
- Manage differences

Developing good relationships with clients or customers shouldn't be something we do when we need something!

Building relationships in business is a continual process of staying in touch with those people, organisations, and contacts we need to keep our business ticking over. How we do this can make or break the link we are trying to forge between ourselves and our clients/customers and prospective clients/customers; and these relationships can be the difference between success and failure in our businesses.

TOP TIP

Never underestimate the power of relationships in business

IMPROVING YOUR COMMUNICATION

- Consider all the factors that affect your communication in a particular situation.
- Adapt your communication to suit your co-communicators' frame of reference.
- Be mindful of assumptions in communication, avoid stereotyping.
- Be aware of non-verbal and paralanguage aspects of communication.
- Be open, flexible and reflexive – observe a video of yourself communicating with others.
- Seek feedback from your peers.

Theories of Communication

Oxford Press – Rola Ajjawi and Charlotte Rees 2005

'*T*o business that we love
we rise betime,
And go to 't with delight.'

William Shakespeare (1564-1616)
Anthony and Cleopatra, IV,4,20

*H*ow people do things is often determined by what they consider to be important in their culture, so the way of communicating can reflect the values and beliefs of a culture.

Culture often determines the way messages are transmitted; and even received! - for example; computers, written material, verbal and non-verbal. Styles also play a part – such as extreme politeness, taboos on who speaks to whom, and non-verbals.

Interacting with others from different cultures can cause some barriers due to different cultural understandings, languages, and styles.

General rules about communication:
◇ We are always communicating.
◇ We perceive things differently.
◇ We can see things that do not exist.
◇ We do not see things that do exist.
◇ How this happens is often determined by our cultural background.

Inter-cultural communication can be successful if:
◇ People have open attitudes towards other cultures.
◇ General good communication skills are practised.
◇ Status of persons involved is similar.
◇ Cultural views are similar.
◇ Knowledge of each other is similar.

Think on all the cultures you may meet in your working week and how they differ from your own.

How should you relate to these variances so as to bring about the results you wish for your company or organisation?

Let us look at some Top Tips that may shorten our study of understanding of cultures not our own:

TOP TIPS:

- Don't assume others will think the way you do
- Don't assume others will understand what you are saying or in fact, doing
- Before conversing with others from different cultures think on how they may converse
- It is not difficult to study other cultures and their ways of communication
- Always be led by the other culture if you are unsure

I have deliberately not given you examples of how other cultures react with each other as well as with us, as the examples would be endless, and immeasurably variable.

I strongly suggest you have someone in your company, organisation or business, do an analysis on those cultures you need to deal with to ascertain what protocols are required.

TOP TIP

Cultural awareness improves our understanding of others

Chapter 3

Management Interaction
A Manager's Communication
Conflict Resolution Principles
Handling Difficult Behaviours in Meetings
Negotiation Strategies

'*T*he only way to develop
responsibility in people
is to give them
responsibility.'

The One Minute Manager Meets the Monkey

*T*he Australian Oxford Dictionary tells us that a *"Manager is a person who is in charge of the affairs of a business etc."*

What it doesn't explain is the *How to do it*.

Gone are the days (well we would think so) when managers sat in their closed office and issued directions through their secretary and memos. Today, most managers are out in the workplace conversing with their staff. Well we hope so!

We have General Managers, Sales Managers, Office Managers, Division Managers, Team Managers, and various other types of managers, and though their roles or job specifications may differ, they all have one thing in common - they have people they need to relate to. How they do this can be the difference between success for the organisation/company or failure!

As a manager, it is worth every effort to communicate well with all staff, from floor level to upper management.

Read through the following suggestions and Top Tips and see where you can improve your communication with your staff and/ or employees because, after all, they are your most important resource.

Some years back a CEO client rang me urgently; it seems the staff were very critical of one employee who wasn't following their rules, and I was called in to settle the discord.

> *This particular employee's office was situated just behind the reception area and he was constantly interrupted to handle visitors at the front desk. He also had the temerity to come in late some mornings and leave early on some afternoons. The staff cried foul and insisted he be 'laid off.' On assessment it turned out that this staffer disliked dealing with people; he was an introvert and worked many hours from his home office and felt he was more than meeting the company requirements. Management insisted*

he was a valued employee and that he stay. The answer was simple – move his office to a secluded position where it didn't interfere with other staff. Everyone was happy.

Your employee (*also refer Staff in Business Relationships*)

Do you know what the staff or employees think about the company? If not, ask them, or give them a questionnaire to fill out (anonymous).

- ◇ Do you know what the employee/staff member thinks about you?
- ◇ What does each employee think about his/her job?
- ◇ Most employees like to feel needed and/or appreciated.
- ◇ Do employees feel free to make complaints and/or suggestions?
- ◇ Most employees like to have input.

Your personal communication

Encourage staff/employees to express their thoughts with you. Personalising your communication so each person feels you have an interest in them shows you care.

- ◇ Talk with employees about what interests them.
- ◇ Ensure each employee has the opportunity to talk with you about problems related to themselves and/or the job.
- ◇ Give praise freely.
- ◇ When criticising work done, use praise first, give the lesson, and finish with a word or two of confidence in them.
- ◇ Listen; observe.

Your actions

Do you discuss with employees their job description? Quite often your employee may not have seen or heard of their job description since their interview.

- ◇ Keep employees informed on actions taken, and why.
- ◇ Explain to employees/staff members why their suggestions and ideas cannot be used.
- ◇ Ensure your instructions are clear and adequate.
- ◇ Ensure the importance of the line of command is recognised.

◇ Never criticise an employee in front of other employees.
◇ Discuss together an employee's 'job review sheet' / 'annual performance appraisal'.
◇ Ensure any decisions made are followed up.
◇ Listen; observe.

Your management style

It's a good idea to re-examine the effectiveness of your interaction with employees regularly. Asking them for feedback should ensure you are getting it right.

◇ Endeavour to resolve any issues between employees as soon as issues arise.
◇ Recognise achievement.
◇ Consider improved procedures with a view to what they offer you in communicating with your employees.
◇ Celebrate milestones and successes.
◇ Have a social secretary.
◇ Take the time to find out the real reason why an employee leaves.

Overall

Work on empowering your employees to feel the success of the organisation is something they are involved in.

TOP TIPS:

- Delegate; show your staff you have confidence in them
- Assist them to feel ownership of their role within the organisation
- Create an atmosphere within the workplace that is conducive to your employees and staff feeling confident, valued and happy

The results of encompassing good interaction throughout your establishment will show in your profit and loss sheet. When employees and staff are happy to come to work, it shows in their output; and happy employees connect well with customers and clients; and happy clients tell other would-be clients.

A happy workplace creates a positive energy that is contagious

CASE STUDY:
Purposeful Communication

A Manager in a large organisation wishes to prevent time-wasting at morning tea breaks. She tries out a number of noticeboard messages and asks you to pick the one most likely to produce worker cooperation.

The messages are:

1. Staff are asked to respect the morning tea privilege. All departments to note.
2. Morning tea is taking too long. Staff late back to work will lose this privilege.
3. Boys and girls, we know you like to chinwag at morning tea break, but give us a break and cut yours down to the allocated 15 minutes provided.
4. A short respite from the morning's work is provided between 10.30 and 10.45 am. Staff are inclined however, to presume on our generosity in the granting of this privilege, with the result that many do not resume normal duties for up to half an hour after the commencement of the break. The rest of the department may be inconvenienced as a result. It is desired that staff take cognisance of the need to cooperate in this regard.
5. Staff are asked to limit their morning tea break to the 15 minutes provided between 10.30 and 10.45 am.

Which of the above do you think would bring the desired result? Or do you have a better one?

*T*he principles which are commonly used for resolving conflict are mainly called upon to settle disputes that occur in teams. However, as a Manager it is wise to be conversant with this process for settling any conflict (either within a team or between individuals) within your organisation.

Every person has distinctive viewpoints that are equally valid (from where they stand) as to the other party's viewpoints involved in any conflict.

Consequently each person's viewpoint makes a contribution to the whole and requires consideration and respect in order to form a complete solution.

This wider view can open up the communication transaction possibilities.

The Six Principles

Step 1: Welcome differences

◇ Find something positive in every divergent view.
◇ Incorporate all statements into team discussion.
◇ Document all comments on flipcharts and/or whiteboards.
◇ Recognise, don't avoid, frustrated team members.

Step 2: React positively

◇ Create a safe place for team members to air differences.
◇ Keep a positive attitude in the face of conflict.
◇ Demonstrate belief in teamwork by always being constructive.
◇ Patiently but assertively moderate discussion, including venting.

Step 3: Use empathy

◇ Listen visibly, actively, and as an ally.

◇ Ensure everyone feels that their voice is heard.

◇ Consciously focus on the ideas and feelings of others.

◇ Try to see things from others' points of view.

Step 4: Use positive feedback

◇ Use recognition, and "I" statements.

◇ Focus on the situation, not the person.

◇ Coach by being direct, specific, assertive, firm and helpful.

◇ Use accepting body language to show clearly that others count.

◇ Balance everything you do with sincere validation.

Step 5: Confront problems

◇ Explore differences by discussing all sides openly.

◇ Find root causes, not symptoms, to find permanent solutions.

◇ Take personal responsibility whether it's your problem or not.

◇ Turn all conflict situations into learning opportunities.

Step 6: Negotiate solutions together

◇ Negotiate win-win situations using collaboration.

◇ Use ground rules to find joint answers.

◇ Use the team's creativity to brainstorm alternatives.

◇ Facilitate group decision-making by seeking consensus.

◇ Build ownership by letting the team solve its own problems.

Evaluate the conflict

◇ Following conflict, it is a good idea to talk with the other person/s concerned to ascertain their thinking regarding the process.

◇ Think about how the conflict played out and if you could improve how you handle it in the future.

Ways to use the Conflict Resolution Principles

This method can be used even when the other person or persons are not using this method.

TOP TIPS:

- By listening with respect and speaking briefly in non-inflammatory ways, we can help the other person/s to calm down and engage in a more productive discussion
- When you are involved in a dispute or feel an argument is brewing, you could explain the method briefly and ask the other person to join you in trying this way of relating
- You could introduce the method when things are calm and peaceful. In a family meeting, class session, or work gathering, we could explain that conflict is often inevitable in any group and this method could help you and the person/s involved to discuss differences in a positive and productive way

Another way of using the conflict resolution method is to assist others to resolve their differences by acting as the third party, and remaining neutral to ensure the method is followed.

TOP TIP

Establishing procedures for handling disputes can alleviate conflict

'*I*n a world of finite men, conflict is inevitably associated with creativity.

Without conflict there is no major personal change or social progress.

On the other hand, runaway conflict (as in modern war) can destroy what men intended to save by it.

Conflict management then becomes crucially important.

This involves accepting or even encouraging such conflict as is necessary,

but at the same time doing everything possible to keep it to the minimum essential to change,

to confine it to the least destructive forms,

and to resolve it as rapidly and constructively as possible.'

Harvey Seifert, social scientist, and
Howard Clinebell, Jr., pastoral counsellor.

Meetings, meetings, and more meetings; they're a reality of life for many of us! Business Meetings, P&C Meetings, Club Meetings, Community Meetings, you name it, if there is a group of people doing something, you can rely on the fact that they will have meetings.

Obviously there are things to be discussed, agendas to be followed, ideas to be put forward, decisions to be made. But do we always get heard? Or do we get talked over and/or down? Does the loudest voice win?

When involved in group discussions, especially if you are the leader or chairperson, watch for various common types of behaviours that can create barriers to effective communication.

Following are the most common you will come across, with some suggestions as to how to deal with them so that meetings can be productive.

Overly Talkative Types
These people will keep talking over everyone else, and tend to monopolize the entire conversation.

How to handle
  ◇ Summarise the major points made and turn discussion back to the group.
  ◇ Ask them closed questions, to which they can only answer 'yes' or 'no.'

Silent Types
These people tend to be shy, reserved and rarely offer any comments, even to open questions.

How to handle

- ◇ Include them in the discussion.
- ◇ Encourage them to participate.
- ◇ Support their ideas.
- ◇ Ask open-ended questions.
- ◇ Follow your questions with an expectant, friendly look, listen actively, give minimal encouragers.

Crabby Types

These people will find fault with everything - the heating, the seating, the subject, the other persons attending.

How to handle

- ◇ Acknowledge their complaints and determine if complaints are legitimate.
- ◇ If complaints can be corrected, have them suggest solutions.
- ◇ Get feedback from the group.
- ◇ If complaints aren't justified, suggest they reserve judgment until session is finished.

Know-It-Alls

These people think they are experts concerning the subject at hand, and will speak out to give their views. If not interrupting the person speaking they will mumble their thoughts to those around them.

How to handle

- ◇ Avoid getting into any argument.
- ◇ Try and promote a win-win situation without discrediting you or them.
- ◇ Acknowledge the main points they have raised.
- ◇ Thank them for their contribution.

General Conflict

Occasionally, disruptive people can cause argument and debate between those attending, and this can lead to the meeting descending into chaos.

How to handle

◇ Quickly step in and play arbitrator before the situation escalates.

◇ Concentrate on points of agreement.

◇ Emphasise the importance of ideas rather than personalities.

◇ If dragging on, or taking too much time, call for a break, or suggest discussion be continued at a later time.

TOP TIPS:

- Be aware of the type of behaviour
- Listen carefully – don't cut in
- Use the same demeanour you normally have
- Acknowledge the complaint
- Summarize point/s made
- Avoid argument
- Move discussion to a later time or date if necessary

Participants who are disruptive in meetings have a detrimental impact that reaches further into the organisation than just the meeting or meetings they attend. It is very advisable that the disruptive person is spoken to one-on-one, remembering not to attack the person, but speak to the behaviour and its consequences.

As for other personality behaviour types, it is worthwhile remembering that "together everyone achieves more" and to always include them in proceedings. You may be surprised at their level of input!

TOP TIP

Stay focused and 'keep your cool'

Hints for dealing with difficult people

*L*isten.
Try to see things from their point of view.
Hear them out.
Recognize their style of communication.
Refrain from judgment.
Listen some more.
Clarify their concerns if necessary.
Be patient.
Let them talk until they run out of argument.
Use assertive skills.
Tell them you understand.
Reflect on your own communication.

*T*he Oxford Dictionary tells us that to negotiate is to: *"Try to reach an agreement, compromise, or arrangement by discussion. Get over or through an obstacle or difficulty successfully."*

Negotiation can also be described as 'bargaining' and even 'trading.'

It can appear to be complicated, especially as we hear of countries having to settle their differences through 'negotiation.'

Actually, we ourselves regularly use negotiation tactics. We usually negotiate a price when purchasing property; we might negotiate to buy household items at a price that suits our budget; we probably have had to negotiate our salary or wages. Negotiation might even come into play to decide who does the washing up!

Negotiation is all about coming to an agreement that satisfies the needs of the parties concerned. We may have to lose a little of what we want to gain, a little of what we need, and presumably the other party will also have to lose a little of what they want to gain, a little of what they need. This style of negotiation is called a 'win-win' situation, and gives each party an agreement which both parties can live or work with. A win-win outcome is the target of good negotiation.

Win-win requirements
To achieve a win-win result, be prepared to give up something from your side of the equation. Build trust by being able to be relied upon. Keep your word.

Explain your side of the issue honestly and clearly.

⬦ Show respect for other views. Value not only your own arguments but those of the other person.

⬦ Be co-operative and prepared to work with the other person/s to address the problem or issues.

⬦ Have empathy. What does the issue look like from the other side?

◇ Show that you care about different views.

◇ Have the attitude of "together we can achieve more."

Strategies

Stay focused on the end objective. Know what your 'walk-away' or 'bottom line' is. Modify your personal style if necessary to get results.

◇ Try to understand the other person/s personality style/s.

◇ Be honest. The other party needs to know you can be trusted.

◇ Build rapport. Match the style of your communication to that used by the other party.

Have a 'fall back' strategy. Can you reduce your up-front figure or argument?

Personality Styles in negotiation

Our style of communication, as well as the communication style of shall we say, our adversaries, is most important when in a negotiation scenario.

Our style is made up of our attitudes, values, prejudices and fears. Others may not remember what we wear or even what we say, but they will remember our behaviour and how we interacted with them.

Knowing the style of communication you mostly use; (the main four being - dominant, friendly, expressive or cautious), observe the style of others in the negotiation process. This will allow you to modify your style to suit the other person, or group.

For instance, if you are the friendly, calm, people-oriented style, you may find it difficult to say no or stand up for what it is you want.

◇ If you are the dominant style, you may need to pull back a little from the 'get the task done' attitude to suit the style of others.

◇ Similarly, the expressive style of person may find it difficult to relate to others who don't share their 'big picture' style of communication.

◇ With the cautious style of personality, problems can arise if they are too cautious and fail to move forward in the negotiation process.

Our style can have a great impact on others, so we need to be aware of how we relate in conflict and especially when negotiating an outcome.

Negotiating with difficult personalities

Every person sees things from a different perspective. They probably have a different frame of reference, so try and understand what it is exactly they would be happy with.

◇ You could show interest by asking appropriate questions.

◇ Follow the other's style of communication.

◇ Use self-assertive skills.

◇ Practice patience.

◇ Don't allow yourself to be roused to anger.

◇ Self disclose if necessary – let the other person know where you are coming from.

◇ Check if you yourself are perhaps a 'difficult' person to deal with.

◇ Confront negative behaviour. (That is, the behaviour, not the person!)

◇ Meet inflexibility with compromise.

◇ Show a friendly demeanour.

◇ Find common ground.

TOP TIPS:

Here are four win-win methods with actions designed to replace competitive or contrary bargaining:

Build Working Relationships by

- Seeking common ground
- Separating people from problems

Do not:

- Search for weaknesses in your opponents
- Look for advantages over your opponents
- Attack opponents

Explore Options for Mutual Gain by

- Openly laying out the 'needs' of yourself and the other person/s
- Sharing information

Do not:

- Bargain, haggle, and horse-trade
- Make concessions you won't keep

Satisfy Both Sets of Interests by

- Considering objective merits
- Basing decisions on principle

Do not:

- Employ leverage
- Base actions on manipulation

Solve Each Other's Problems by

- Using wide-open creative thinking

Do not:

- Limit thinking, dig in, or close your mind
- Use ultimatums

Win-Win Negotiating Process for Teams

When dealing with a team situation, using the following process should bring a favourable result:

a. **Present -** one at a time. Present your reality completely while the other person/s, listen. Acknowledge, and interrupt only to clarify understanding.
b. **Agree** – together. Find, discuss, and list areas of agreement; common goals, interests, values, and views.
c. **Disagree** - As the discussion progresses, identify key issues of disagreement that keep coming up or interfering with agreement.

Narrow your key differences to the top one or two. Discuss them in depth to understand each other's views, and define the exact problem.

d. **Negotiate** - Discuss and explore potential ways to resolve your differences, each trying to solve the other's problem in a way you can each live with. Consider and evaluate all of your options until you find a mutually acceptable solution. Then agree on steps needed to make it work.

Negotiation is a skill that really isn't difficult to learn for our everyday living and working situations – and the rewards are enormous. If you find it hasn't worked the first time you try, don't despair. Try again – and again – and again.

As in all interactive situations where conflict, differences of opinion, or different needs arise, it is never a good idea to try these skills if you are in a bad mood, holding a grudge, or are tired. Time your communication with a positive attitude and things will go much better.

It has been said that "All things are negotiable." The trick is to negotiate an outcome where most persons involved are satisfied with the result.

TOP TIP

Negotiation can allay discord

'*W*hen a man tells me he's going to put all his
cards on the table,
I always look up his sleeve.'

Lord Howe-Belisha

Chapter 4

Leadership Interaction
Leadership Communication
Teamwork
Handling Team Conflict
Collaborative Problem Solving

*'E*veryone is a potential
high Performer.
Some people just need
a little help
along the way.'

Leadership and the One Minute Manager
Kenneth Blanchard, Ph.D.
Patricia Zigarmi, Ed.D.
Drea Zigarmi, Ed.D.

*I*s leadership inborn or can it be learned?

The Defence Forces describe leadership as: "The art of influencing a body of people to follow a certain course of action; the art of controlling them, directing them and getting the best out of them. A major part of leadership is man-management."

There is always one person in a group who will have the confidence to step up and lead – either for good or for bad. They have the demeanour of confidence. Often that confidence is all they need to be a great and even inspiring leader who others will gladly follow. Obviously they would have other characteristics as well in varying degrees, such as: social qualities which make him/her popular, a humane-nature, or certain skills pertaining to the role they play – but confidence is the main ingredient.

However, many leadership skills, including communication skills, can be learned and practised.

There are two different types of Leadership: Formal Authority and Earned Authority.

Formal Authority – has a formal title or rank that commands respect and attention. People follow these leaders because they are 'the leader.'

Earned Authority – this authority is 'informal' or 'earned' from personal relationships built with others. These people are considered by others to be leaders because they can help achieve goals.

In all cases, leaders are individuals who know how to influence others. They understand people and know how to use the tools of authority.

Attributes or Qualities of a Leader

If we look at some of these qualities we will find;

◇ Enthusiasm – it may be a quiet and slow-burning enthusiasm, rather than the heat and fireworks of passion, but it will be there.

◇ Integrity – the quality that engenders trust.

◇ Toughness coupled with fairness – people respect a leader with high standards and who will not compromise on them; a leader who is consistent, fair and does not ask from others what they do not require from themselves first.

◇ Humanity – leaders need to exemplify basic humaneness, an inner kindness or empathy when an occasion calls for it.

◇ Confidence – without a level of self-belief, none of us could put our talents to work.

◇ Humility – a readiness to listen and be taught. Willingness to admit when they are wrong. A reverence for others.

◇ Courage – whereas not all physically brave individuals have moral courage, those with moral courage are physically brave as well. Courage of either kind is universally admired, not least in a leader.

Functions of Leadership

It would seem obvious I think that one of the first functions of being able to lead is having the ability to plan.

◇ What is your **plan?** Gather all the information you need to bring together your purpose or goal. Can you define your group task? Put together a workable plan.

◆ **Initiating** – you need to be able to brief your group on your aims and the plan; explaining why it's necessary and how it will work; allocating tasks; setting standards.

◆ **Controlling** – maintaining standards. Influencing tempo. Ensuring all actions are taken towards objectives.

- ◇ **Supporting** – expressing acceptance of each person's contribution. Encouraging group and individuals. Disciplining group/individuals as necessary. Creating team spirit. Reconciling disagreements or getting others to explore them.
- ◇ **Informing** – clarifying task and plan. Giving new information to the group, keeping them in the picture. Receiving information from the group. Summarising suggestions and ideas coherently.
- ◇ **Evaluating** – checking feasibility of an idea. Testing consequences of a proposed solution. Evaluating group performance. Helping the group to evaluate its own performance.

Team Leaders

- ◇ Need to be able to communicate how the goals set will be reached.
- ◇ Need self-confidence.
- ◇ Need to be able to keep people working together towards a common objective.
- ◇ Create a team. Who will do what? How will they work together?
- ◇ Empower the team to express themselves.
- ◇ Motivate the team by identifying successes on the way.
- ◇ Actively listen to ideas.
- ◇ Make the appropriate decisions.
- ◇ Create hope for the future.

Note: *With no true leader, personal agendas can take over and often teams can lose their way.*

LEADERSHIP STYLES

There are commonly four leadership styles:

Directing – leader provides specific instructions and closely supervises task accomplishments.

Coaching – leader continues to direct and closely supervise task accomplishment, but also explains decisions, solicits suggestions, and supports progress.

Supporting – leader facilitates and supports the team's efforts toward task accomplishment and shares responsibility for decision-making with them.

Delegating – leader turns over responsibility for decision making and problem solving to the team.

LEADERSHIP IN ACTION

If you are the Leader, the following suggestions will show you what your action should look like. You will be required to:

- Establish vision and values.
- Set direction and goals. Show how to attain.
- Delegate effectively.
- Persuade others.
- Project confidence.
- Communicate the big picture to team, as well as one-on-one.
- Support team members.
- Keep informed on progress.
- Develop people. Coach others.
- Build team spirit.
- Give praise and appreciation. Recognise success.
- Respect ideas and opinions.

10 TOP TIPS ON LEADERSHIP

1. Lead democratically
2. Accept advice
3. Be approachable
4. Listen
5. Respect other views

6. Be informed
7. Have courage
8. Delegate
9. Keep all team members in the loop
10. Coach team members as necessary

You may now realise that leadership can in fact be learned.

Leaders know the difference between being the 'boss' to being the 'leader.' For example, when the team does well, the 'boss' will take the credit, whereas the 'leader' gives the credit to the team! When things don't go well, the 'boss' will blame the team, whereas the 'leader' blames him or herself.

Bear in mind effective leaders also realise that interacting with those whom they lead is of paramount importance, and that's where the skills of communication with others comes into play. Leaders work on having good people skills. They maintain a positive attitude to lead and empower others.

TOP TIP

Inspiring leaders understand people

'**W**hen the best leader's work is done,
the people say,
"We Did It Ourselves!"'

Leadership and the One Minute Manager
Kenneth Blanchard Ph.D.

Before teams came along, most workers had to choose between doing what the boss said (even if the boss was wrong!) or speaking up and being labelled a 'trouble-maker.'

Today, most companies and/or organisations work in teams, and teams can provide many benefits not only to the organisation, but to each person within a team. We can learn skills such as leadership, management, people skills, delegation, problem solving, conflict resolution, negotiation and empowerment.

All teams need to be united around a common goal; they need to be able to work together, share responsibility, depend on each other, and be empowered to implement consensus decisions. How we perform within this team environment will be noticed by those in positions of power and can often lead to further career advancement.

The following suggestions and Top Tips may inspire you to improve your performance in working within a team. You may also find an idea or two that you can introduce to your team.

Team Members Main Functions

- ◇ As a team member we should be an active player. Politeness is good; silence when you have an opinion and feelings, isn't.
- ◇ Willingly share responsibility for the teams' work.
- ◇ Collect input before team meetings.
- ◇ Contribute information and expertise during meetings.
- ◇ Represent the team to customers, suppliers, and co-workers.
- ◇ Keep commitments.
- ◇ Delegate to another team member if we cannot keep a commitment.
- ◇ Ask for help if we have a problem.

Supporting the Team

- ◇ Help define charter, plans, ground rules, and action steps.
- ◇ Follow the team's road map (hopefully they have one), plans, and ground rules.
- ◇ Understand team roles and take responsibility seriously.
- ◇ Get to know other team members and cooperate fully.
- ◇ Help resolve team problems and internal differences.

Representing the Team

- ◇ Make frequent personal contacts with stakeholders.
- ◇ Keep outsiders informed about team progress.
- ◇ Contribute to written reports.
- ◇ Actively participate in team presentations.

Be involved

- ◇ Review team meeting minutes.
- ◇ Complete actions and follow through commitments on time.
- ◇ Collect input and gather information about team proposals.
- ◇ Meet with team leader or other members as needed.
- ◇ Prepare to participate fully and be on time for all meetings.

TOP TIPS:

Be proactive

- Offer special knowledge and expertise
- Think creatively and use brainstorming tools
- Communicate, listen openly, and help build consensus
- Recognise others contribution and encourage feedback

Team Life Cycles

Recognising that all teams have a life cycle and go through phases helps us understand at what level the team is performing.

Phase 1. Team Direction

Define team direction with a mission statement.

Phase 2. Team Organisation

Begins when you are asked to join the team; before you get too deeply involved, make sure you and your teammates have the resources necessary to achieve success.

Phase 3. Team Building
Getting to know each other and learning to work together.

Phase 4. Teamwork
Real progress can be made when you reach this phase. You will talk with people outside meetings, run experiments, meet frequently.

Phase 5. Continuous Improvement
This stage reviews a team's progress, troubleshoots obstacles and helps one another.

Phase 6. Wrap Up
Some teams go on forever, but if you are working on a project, you'll need to conclude effectively. That means evaluating results, documenting findings, reporting to those concerned and recognising those who contributed.

Working Together

- ◊ Good teamwork depends on working with others and helping each other to succeed.
- ◊ Cooperation and communication becomes all-important.
- ◊ We need to understand, get along with, and respect our teammates.
- ◊ Good team members cover for and support each other without being asked.
- ◊ Spend time and effort building working partnerships.
- ◊ Don't expect to work on a team where everybody is totally compatible.
- ◊ A team of different personality types opens minds.
- ◊ Learning to work with different personalities enhances tolerance.
- ◊ Healthy debate can cause us to look at things from many different angles.
- ◊ Healthy debate is not allowing debate to become personal.
- ◊ Be alert to inheriting conflicts that already exist in the organisation.

Communication styles

There are four communication styles to consider when working with others:

Results oriented – These people like to 'get on with the job' and drive self and others to quick, tangible, and measurable results. They will respond to your communication if you give them straight answers.

Accuracy oriented – This person will always be thinking, analysing forces, and considering events. They like to make sure all the 't's are crossed and the 'i's dotted. If you explain your thinking to them they will be amenable to plans put forward.

Interaction oriented – These are the people who can always see the big picture. They communicate ideas and feelings openly and expressively. Listen and openly express your thoughts to this style of personality.

Harmony oriented – These people find it uncomfortable to work if the atmosphere is discordant. They act agreeable, supportive, and co-operative, and are extra concerned about politeness and positiveness with a harmony driven team mate.

Think about the personality and style of your team-mates before you assume they will think, feel and react as you do!

Cultivating participation
  ◇ Allow teammates to talk and be themselves.
  ◇ Encourage them to share their feelings and reveal hidden agendas.
  ◇ Build mutual trust by allowing them to vent.
  ◇ Recognise and learn to adjust to different social styles.

Resolving differences
  ◇ Welcome and identify conflicts as early as possible.
  ◇ Confront and work through differences.
  ◇ Resolve power and other issues as they occur.
  ◇ Always try to negotiate win-win situations.

Consensus

◇ Input from everyone involved in the team is desirable.
◇ Set goals and directions as a team.
◇ When a consensus from all members cannot be reached, it is left to majority rule.
◇ Team ground rules will help you decide which way will be put into practice.

Contracting

◇ Each team member is committed to contribute to the team as a whole.
◇ Normally this is done verbally.
◇ Some organisations have written contracts between members and other departments who may be involved with the team.

TOP TIPS:

When expectations differ

- Go back to vision, values and strategy of the organisation and/or as the team proposed at the outset
- Evaluate leadership and decision making. Is it participative, consultative or directive? This must be known to all – what type of decision making is to be followed. This is best included when setting ground rules
- Refer to roles and responsibilities
- The nature of reality

There is more to teamwork than just facts and figures, charters and plans. The human element is vital to your success. You need to routinely make time to work on your team chemistry. To function well together as a team, it is necessary to learn to give each other constructive feedback and to work toward and reach consensus.

TOP TIP

Together Everyone Achieves More

'**Y**ou can handle people more successfully
by enlisting their feelings than by
convincing their reason.'

Anonymous

13 Qualities of High Performance Teams

Purpose: A clear, challenging, and inspiring common purpose defined.

Membership: A team that is complete, willing, skilled, available, and trained.

Leadership: Leadership with high standards that builds the team and guides results until the team can take charge.

Structure: A flexible, fully defined, results-oriented structure of roles, processes, and procedures under team control.

Plans: Long-range Master Plans and short-range Action Plans based on an appropriate team road map with measureable milestones.

Participation: Active participation of all team members who pull their fair share and follow through.

Communication: Open communication channels, active listening, and fully informed members.

Trust: Mutual trust, support, and collaboration so that team members back up each other.

Consensus: Critical decisions by consensus, especially when differences produce conflict.

Ownership: Joint ownership and shared responsibility for implementation.

Empowerment: Sufficient empowerment with active external support enabling the team to achieve its mission.

Synergy: High synergy, meaning total team energy is greater than the sum of its individual parts.

Recognition: Appropriate rewards, frequent recognition, and routine celebrations.

Working in Teams, A Team Member Guidebook.
Sandy Pokras, Crisp Publications Inc. California, 1997

CORE INTERPERSONAL SKILLS
10 important skills for the Professional

1. Approachability – open body language
2. Smile – increases your face value
3. Welcoming and greeting – shake hands, be friendly
4. Name – people like to hear their name used
5. Politeness – good manners are always appreciated
6. Respectful language – watch the grammar
7. Praise – we all like a compliment
8. Humour – in good taste only
9. Eye contact – direct but not over-doing it
10. Proximity – stay in your own space

*I*n all teams there is bound to be some amount of conflict. Some of this conflict can be constructive, in that it allows different opinions to be aired and a solution found. It can also be beneficial when it inspires members of the team to produce better results, even think more creatively. However, when it causes discord, it has a profound effect and can cause the team to fall apart.

The best way to deal with conflict is to focus on the Problem, not the people. This can be difficult when someone argues against our favourite proposal, or shoots down what we want to say - but it can be done. It requires patience, understanding and recognition that this could be a learning experience for us.

Healthy teams learn to communicate their reactions quickly and constructively. They have an understanding on how to give and receive feedback, how to give positive reinforcement and advice, and how to negotiate until everyone is happy; and then hold each other accountable for agreements made.

Go through the following suggestions and see where your team could improve their handling of conflict. *Also refer to Conflict Resolution Chapter 3.*

Feedback

There are times when feedback is necessary to help a team member, or the team, through conflict. This could be in situations such as:

◊ When they don't seem to understand.
◊ When discussions go off track.
◊ When the person or persons show an attitude that makes others feel uncomfortable.
◊ When a team member behaves in a way that is disruptive to the team.
◊ When someone uses language that the team objects to.
◊ When a forceful personality dominates discussion or grandstands and the team isn't interested.

Most times it is best to give feedback one-on-one; there are times, however, when it is better done with the whole group. Neither method is fun, because people tend to react, but feedback gets easier as team relationships improve.

Positive Reinforcement and Advice one-on-one

Feedback is easier to give and produces a better result when couched in positive reinforcement guidelines, as follows:

◊ Give encouragement. The purpose is to encourage a specific action, behaviour or performance so that it will be repeated.

◊ Keep your feedback pure. Mixing reinforcement with criticism or advice dilutes it and may poison the desired effect.

◊ Be positive. Reinforce what is wanted; concentrate on the positive and ignore undesirable actions.

◊ Be supportive. Support what people are trying to accomplish or what they are having difficulty with.

◊ Be specific. Recognise a specific event or behaviour. General compliments tend to be taken as empty praise.

◊ Be descriptive. Feedback should describe in detail what worked, what was liked, and what was good.

◊ Make it understandable. Be clear in discussion, without technical terms or buzzwords.

◊ Be genuine. Use genuine statements, not canned phrases the same way over and again, or sincerity will be questioned.

◊ Immediacy. Reinforcement is best done as soon as possible after the event or action.

◊ Frequency. Positive feedback following each meeting helps the person concerned until the behaviour/action becomes routine.

◊ Feedback reduction. When all is going well, compliment, encourage, and reduce feedback and advice as necessary.

Whole Team Feedback

◇ Be constructive. Help each other learn and grow. Suggest actions to take.

◇ Be fair. Maintain objectivity and impartiality.

◇ Be honest. Use assertion methods to get your message across, and actual observations of behaviour.

◇ Be specific. Give concrete, meaningful details, backed up with supporting examples.

◇ Be ongoing. Communicate openly and give interim feedback.

TOP TIPS:
Feedback negatives

Avoid being

- Destructive. Keep away from 'put downs,' ganging up or hatchet jobs
- Negative - including whining and complaining
- Judgemental; or giving off-the-cuff comments and blanket generalities

Accepting feedback

- Listen carefully and try to see things from the other's point of view
- Breathe deeply and stay calm
- Clarify, using questions to make sure you understand
- Acknowledge what you hear and understand without arguing
- Sort out what you've heard and decide what you can agree with

Differences are to be expected in a group of different personalities, different backgrounds, different education etc.

Disruptions can come about through these differences; people can feel friction and discomfort; the team becomes distracted, wastes time, and looses the impetus to succeed.

Conflict becomes common place. Built up tensions can explode with meetings getting out of control, which causes permanent damage to relationships.

These differences, disruptions and general conflict can bring about the failure of the team, and it may be necessary to go to the formal Conflict Resolution Principles to help handle the friction that has occurred.

Conflict resolution

If you and/or the team are involved in communication breakdown, you could follow the conflict resolution principles – see chapter 3.

If conflict continues, go back to:

1. Formal issues.
2. Get rid of personal issues.
3. Get rid of assumptions.

Team members are obviously going to be naturally different. Many teams purposely recruit members with built-in differences, with the hope that the team members will work them out. As a result, tension within teams is expected. Most gradually overcome these frictions and become productive. But if team members solely focus on themselves instead of *the team,* progress will be difficult to achieve.

If you are involved in communication breakdown, endeavour not to take it personally. Concentrate on the problem and/or situation, not the person. By following the conflict resolution principles, you should be able to move forward.

A team that is working well together is a delight to be involved in, creating an atmosphere that goes beyond just their team but the whole organisation.

TOP TIP

Deal with the problem, not the person

'People experiencing conflict tend to respond on the basis of their perceptions of the situation, rather than an objective review of it.

Subsequently, people filter their perceptions (and reactions) through their values, culture, beliefs, information, experience, gender, and other variables.

Conflict responses are both filled with ideas and feelings that can be very strong and

powerful guides to our sense of

possible solutions.'

Healey, 1995.

King Solomon and Collaborative Problem Solving

One day two women came before Solomon
each claiming a child as their own.
The first said, "My Lord, this woman and I share the same house,
and I gave birth to a child when she was there with me.
On the third day after my baby was born,
she too gave birth to a child.

No one else was there with us in the house...
During the night her child died because she lay on it.
Then she arose in the middle of the night and took my child from
my side while I slept, and laid the child in her bosom
and put her dead child in my own bosom.
Thus when I rose toward morning to nurse my child, behold,
it was dead;
but when I was able to examine it closely in the morning light,
it was not my son which I had borne.

The other woman said, "No, the living child belongs to me.
The dead child is yours.
But the first woman was saying at the same time,
"No, the dead child
belongs to you, the living child is mine!"

Thus they wrangled before the king.

The king mused, then he said, "Fetch me a sword."
They brought in a sword and the king gave the order:
"Cut the living child in two and give half to one
and half to the other."

At this the mother of the living child,
whose heart yearned for her boy, cried to the king,
"Oh my Lord, give her the living child, never kill it!"
The other woman said, "No, divide it; neither of us shall have it."

The king said, "Give yonder woman the living child
and by no means slay it, for she is its mother."

Solomon, King of Israel 9th Century B.C.

One of the 5 skills for effective communication, (the others being listening, assertiveness, resolving conflict and choosing which skill to use), problem solving can be used with success in many situations.

The Collaborative Problem Solving Method has proved to be beneficial in dealing with areas of conflict that are 'needs' based.

Other conflict situations can be emotional needs not being met, which can be resolved using conflict resolution methods (*Top Tips for Interpersonal Communication*), and values driven conflict, which can also be resolved using conflict resolution methods.

Once we have established that the conflict in question is not emotional or values driven needs, the conflict that remains can then be settled using collaborative problem solving techniques.

A Collaborative Problem Solving Method can be used to –

◇ Solve personal problems.
◇ Solve business problems.
◇ Resolve social conflict.
◇ Do critical thinking about scientific and other subjects.

There are **6 steps** to the Collaborative Problem Solving Method:

Step 1: Define the problem in terms of needs, not solutions.

An accurate statement of the problem should precede the other steps of problem solving. A haphazard definition of the problem will undermine the entire process.

Step 2: Brainstorm possible solutions.

Brainstorming is defined as the rapid generation and listing of solution ideas without clarification and without evaluation of their merits. Try for quantity not quality.

Step 3: Select the solution (or combination of solutions) that will best meet all parties needs.

If clarification is necessary on some of the solutions that emerged in the brainstorming, this is the time to do it. Once a solution has been reached, try to foresee any possible consequences.

Step 4: Plan who will do what, and by when.

At times, determining the how is also necessary. Specify times when those involved will check how the solution is going. It may also be desirable to write out the agreement reached, including the details of who will do what by when.

Step 5: Implement the plan.

When discussion is completed the parties usually separate to do their part of the agreed upon plan. If a party does not live up to their part of the agreement, then an assertion message, followed by reflective listening, may be needed.

Step 6: Evaluate the problem-solving process.

Assess each of the steps and, at a later date, how well the solution turned out.

Toward the end of the problem-solving session, make sure a time is set to see how the solution is working. If an action plan is not working, it should be corrected, or a new one instituted. If it is working well, celebrate!

TOP TIPS:
Crucial Preliminaries

- Deal with strong feelings first. If you or the other person/s has a strong emotional attachment to the problem it will be difficult to come to a resolution
- Be sure the right people are involved. The people who should be there are those affected by the outcome
- Negotiate a time and place in which to do the problem solving
- Establish ground rules

- Qualify the problem
- Explain the method and why you are using it. If others involved are resistant, use reflective listening to enable them to express themselves, reduce their anxiety and develop trust

Problem solving as an everyday skill

The Collaborative Problem Solving Method can be used in various circumstances. For example:

At Meetings: When setting agendas, procedures, dealing with processes and/or problems arising.

***When setting ground rules and/or behaviours* for family, work and certain social gatherings:** If the persons affected by these rules or behaviours are involved in the process they will be more inclined to follow them.

Goal setting: The problem solving process will help clarify results required and how to go about achieving them.

Interpersonal skills: Assisting others to work out solutions to their questions, problems or concerns for themselves. This is far more effective than 'telling' them the answer.

In dealing with problems, it is most important to deal with the emotional elements first. If you find the process hasn't worked, go back over the steps, checking that the preliminaries are/were in place, and that you have covered each step.

Problem solving is a valuable skill. Use it with other communication skills (i.e. listening, assertiveness, conflict resolution) and your effectiveness in the workplace, and at home, will improve dramatically. Becoming adept with using this method increases our decision making abilities, resulting in an increased awareness of ourselves and those with whom we work, socialise and live with.

TOP TIP

Think of problems as opportunities to learn

'When two elephants fight, it is
The grass underneath that suffers.'

African Proverb

Statistics show that a large portion of our lives is spent in a work environment. That being the case, I believe that if we are happy in that environment this will flow through to our personal and social life.

In any business there will be times when interacting with other employees, customers or clients, even the boss, just doesn't go well. Even though this might ring alarm bells, is it a reason to quit? Probably not! But it does remind us to look at our colleagues and our own personality profiles to help us understand if clashes are coming from this area.

I am often told by managers and staff that such and such a problem has been caused by 'personality clashes,' and that's just the way it is. But is it? Why not study those clashes and see if an adjustment to styles can bring about a positive result. I should add that these 'personality clashes' are usually given as the main reason community groups spend inordinate amounts of time squabbling.

Sometimes all it takes for us to interact more inclusively with others is to change our mindset; think of issues a little differently.

There will be occasions when it's just not worth the effort to 'get along with others', but if you are in business, I'm afraid it's a necessity if the business is to thrive.

∞

'I am the Master of my Fate
I am the Captain of my Soul.'

Excerpt from Invictus Poem by William Ernest Henley

*E*motional Awareness Questionnaire

Answer the following questions by circling Y for yes, N for no or NS for not sure.

1A. I can be around people who are suffering physical pain without getting upset about it.

Y   N   NS

1B. I get sweaty palms when I am with people I don't know.

Y   N   NS

1C. I know I have strong feelings, but most of the time I don't know what those feelings are.

Y   N   NS

1D. I am pretty good at knowing what I feel and why.

Y   N   NS

1E. Sometimes other people's feelings are very clear to me and that can be a problem.

Y   N   NS

1F. I can usually handle people who have strong feelings and unload them on me.

Y   N   NS

2A. I am almost always a rational person and have no problems with my emotions.

Y   N   NS

2B. I have been in love and suddenly, inexplicably lost that feeling completely.

Y N NS

2C. I am overwhelmed by bad moods sometimes.

Y N NS

2D. When I have to make an important decision, I usually know how I feel about it; whether to be scared, excited, angry, or some other combination of emotions.

Y N NS

2E. In a competitive situation in which I am winning or clearly superior, I feel sorry for the other person.

Y N NS

2F. When I am in a room full of people, I can tell how the group is feeling – excited, angry, bored or scared.

Y N NS

3A. I very, very rarely cry.

Y N NS

3B. Sometimes when I watch a TV commercial tears come to my eyes, and I don't really understand why.

Y N NS

3C. Sometimes when I am feeling bad, I can't tell if I am scared or angry.

Y N NS

3D. I am a person who sometimes feels shame and guilt.

Y N NS

3E. If I had the opportunity to shoot an animal like a bird, rabbit or deer, I would not be able to do it because I would feel sorry for the animal.

Y   N   NS

3F. I often change the way I act towards another person because I feel it will make things easier between us.

Y   N   NS

4A. I can easily kill a small animal such as a snake or chicken without feeling anything in particular.

Y   N   NS

4B. I am often jumpy and irritable, and I can't help it.

Y   N   NS

4C. I can lie about feelings because I am embarrassed to speak about them.

Y   N   NS

4D. I am aware of having strong feelings of love and joy.

Y   N   NS

4E. I often do things I don't want to because I can't say no.

Y   N   NS

4F. I am good at helping others sort out their emotions because I can understand why they are feeling them.

Y   N   NS

5A. Sometimes when I am with a person who is very emotional, I am surprisingly calm and without feeling.

Y   N   NS

5B. When I am about to interact with people I don't know, I feel sensations like heart palpitations, stomach cramps, dryness in the throat etc

Y   N   NS

5C. Sometimes I am flooded by emotions that disguise and confuse me.

Y   N   NS

5D. From time to time, I am aware of having feelings of anger, from slight irritation to rage.

Y   N   NS

5E. If another person is emotional, I am usually able to tell what emotion they are feeling; such as fear, happiness, sadness, hope or anger.

Y   N   NS

5F. I enjoy situations in which people are having strong positive emotions of love, hope and joy; like at weddings or church services.

Y   N   NS

6A. After a difficult time with another person, I sometimes feel as if parts of my body are numb.

Y   N   NS

6B. I take one or more over-the-counter drugs to deal with headaches, stomach and digestive problems, or bodily pains that my doctor cannot explain.

Y   N   NS

6C. I know I have very strong feelings, but I am frequently unable to discuss them with other people.

Y   N   NS

6D. I am aware of having feelings of fear, ranging from apprehension to terror.

Y   N   NS

6E. Sometimes I can feel other people's feelings in my body.

Y   N   NS

6F. Other people appreciate me because I know how to cool down emotional situations.

Y   N   NS

Scoring: Count the number of YES answers for each of the letters.

A:..........   **B:** ....   **C:** ....

D: ....   **E:** ....   **F:** ....

Interpretations:

A: A greater number of **A** answers can mean that this person can be numb regarding feelings and can be described as cold/blunt.

They are unaware that feelings can physically be felt in their bodies. This is possibly worse in some situations.

This person can often stay calm in crisis situations and can lead a group.

B: A greater number of **B** answers means that these people experience the physical sensations of feelings, e.g. the contracting of muscles in their neck or stomach, but do not realise that they are afraid or angry.

They may not realise that the physical pain they feel has to do with what they are experiencing, e.g. if they have a stress headache they may take medication for the headache, but do nothing about the stress.

They may use or abuse medication in order to control the physical symptoms of their feelings.

C: The person who has more **C** answers than other numbers experiences feelings as heightened levels of energy.

They may not understand them and are unable to talk about them. This person is vulnerable to emotions they may not be able to control; may have emotional outbursts; be impulsive or depressed.

This person is often the first to suffer a setback as a result of stress, and it is important they become emotionally more effective.

To be able to talk about their emotions, they require an environment that is friendly to emotional information. If there is no-one willing to listen to this person's feelings and needs, they will never learn to express them.

Mutual expression of feelings is necessary to enhance emotional awareness.

D: This person is able to recognise different feelings and their intensity and can talk about them.

They understand the difference between basic feelings and realise that they may experience different feelings in the same situation. They are aware that an initial feeling can intensify from angry to furious; that one feeling can lead to another. e.g. hurt then anger.

As this person begins to understand the exact nature of their feelings, they also begin to understand the causes of those feelings; in other words the events that trigger their emotional responses.

They understand that their behaviour can lead to certain feelings in other people.

E: This person is intuitively aware of the different feelings that other people experience.

This is learnt during childhood; some people are naturally empathetic while others are totally unaware of the feelings of others.

Empathy can often be incorrect – for example, you need to ask for confirmation, such as "Do you feel unhappy?" can really mean "No, I am frustrated."

F: In order to reach this level, we need to know how people react to the feelings of others, and whether the interaction will be positive or negative.

It is the most sophisticated level of emotional awareness: to know what you and others feel, and to be able to predict how emotions will influence each other. You can use your emotional awareness to have more comfortable, positive and constructive interactions with others.

*This questionnaire was adapted from *Emotional Intelligence Workbook*, Le Roux & de Klerk.

Notes ....

....

....

....

....

....

....

....

....

Communication Profile - Management

*H*ow's your management communication? Being an effective manager requires interest in your people. Answer the following with a tick or cross to see how you fare, and more importantly, what you can do to improve your management communication.

- ☐ Do you personalise your communication so each person feels you have an interest in them?
- ☐ Do you endeavour to find out what your co-workers really think of you, the company and their job?
- ☐ Do you ensure the importance of the line of command is recognised?
- ☐ Do you encourage employees to express their thoughts to you?
- ☐ Do you give employees the opportunity to talk with you about problems related to themselves or their job?
- ☐ Do you ensure employees can feel free to make complaints?
- ☐ Do you keep employees informed on action taken?
- ☐ Do you ask employees for advice or suggestions regarding your work?
- ☐ Do you explain fully to an employee when their suggestions and ideas cannot be used?
- ☐ Do you take the time to find out the real reason why an employee leaves?
- ☐ Do you re-examine the effectiveness of your communication regularly?
- ☐ Do you consider improved procedures with a view to what they offer you in communicating with your employees?
- ☐ Do you ensure your instructions to employees are clear and adequate?

- ☐ Do you ensure your employees feel at ease when they approach you for help with problems that come up in their work?
- ☐ Do you give reasons for any changes in employee work assignments?
- ☐ Do you avoid criticising employees in the presence of others?
- ☐ Do you talk about things that are of interest to your employees?

Notes ....

....

....

....

....

....

Australian Institute of Professional Counsellors, *Diploma of Professional Counselling.* 2004

Beckett, Wendy. *Blake's Go Guides Better Communication with family, friends and colleagues.* Pascall Press. 2005

Berens Linda V. *Cooper Sue A. Et al. 16 Personality Types in Organisations.* Telos Publications. 2001

Bolton, PH.D. Robert. *People Skills.* Simon Schuster Australia, 1991

Dacosta, Vince. *Influence Persuade and Win.* Vince DaCosta & Associates Inc. Canada 1993

Dr Ronel le Roux & Dr. Rina de Klerk, *Emotional Intelligence.* 2010

Gerson, Richard F Ph.D. *Beyond Customer Service.* Crisp Publications Inc. California. 1992

Hicks, Ph.D. Robert F. Bone, Diane. *Self Managing*

Hill, Napoleon. *Positive Action Plan.* Plume Penquin Group, 1997

Ingham, Gavin DK. *Motivate People.* Dorling Kindersley, London 2007

Institute for Motivational Living Inc. *The Personality System.* Target Training International Ltd. 2001

Laborde, Genie Z. *Influencing with Integrity.* Syntony Publishing, California. 1997

Mackay, Hugh. *Why Don't People Listen?* Pan McMillan Australia, 1994

Martin. Ph.D. William B. *Quality Customer Service.* Crisp Publications Inc. California. 1993

Pokras, Sandy. *Working In Teams.* Crisp Publications Inc. California. 1997

Relationships Australia 2010

Ventrella, Scott W. *The Power of Positive Thinking in Business.* Vermilion. London.2001

www.ingramcontent.com/pod-product-compliance
Lightning Source LLC
Chambersburg PA
CBHW040856220326
41521CB00043B/2600